KIDS SING
PRAISE AND WORSHIP
10 EASY VOCAL SOLOS

To access companion recorded accompaniments online, visit:
www.halleonard.com/mylibrary

Enter Code
1369-9142-3664-2036

ISBN 978-1-4803-5228-5

HAL•LEONARD®
CORPORATION
7777 W. BLUEMOUND RD. P.O. BOX 13819 MILWAUKEE, WI 53213

Visit Hal Leonard Online at
www.halleonard.com

CONTENTS

Pianists on the recordings:
1 Brendan Fox
2 Joshua Parman

As the Deer

Words and Music by
Martin Nystrom

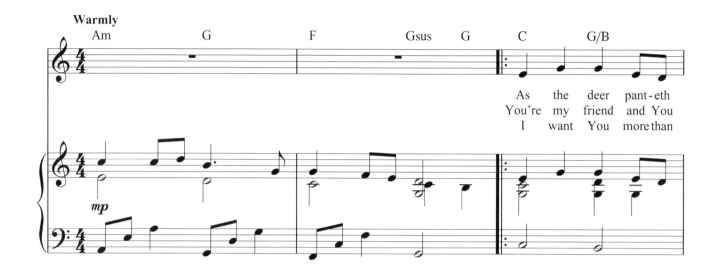

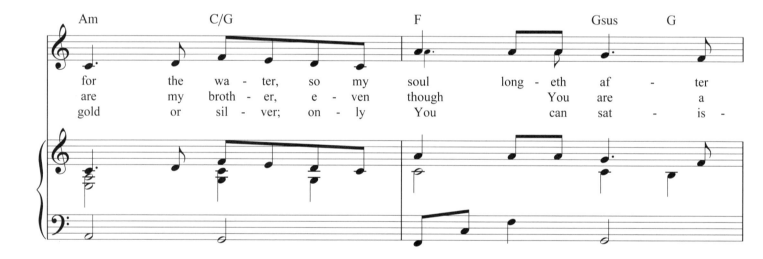

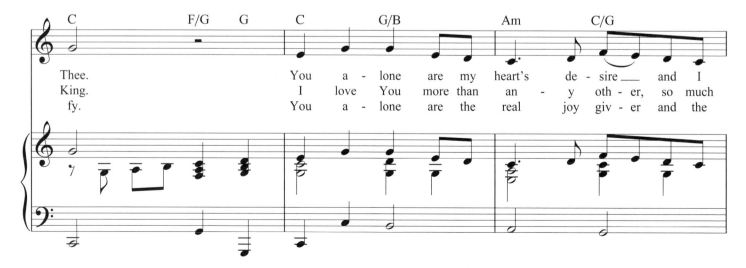

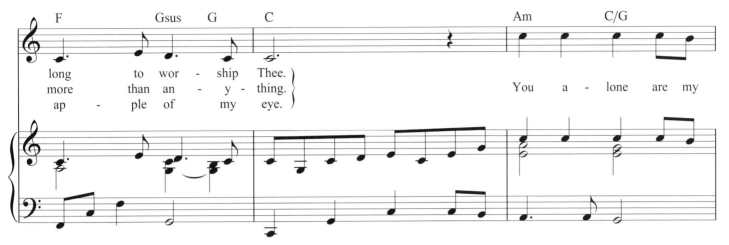

long   to wor - ship Thee.
more   than an - y - thing.
ap - ple of my eye.

You a - lone are my

strength, my shield. To You a - lone may my spir - it

yield.

You a - lone are my heart's de - sire ___ and I

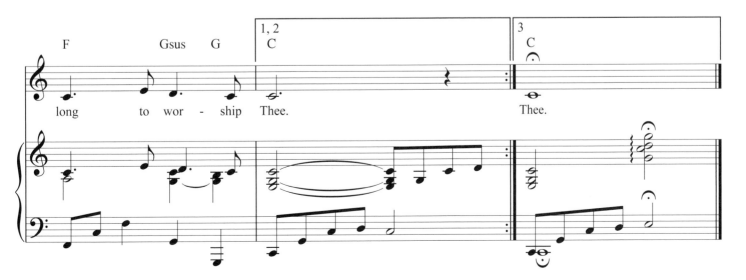

long   to wor - ship Thee.

Thee.

Father, I Adore You

Words and Music by
Terrye Coelho Strom

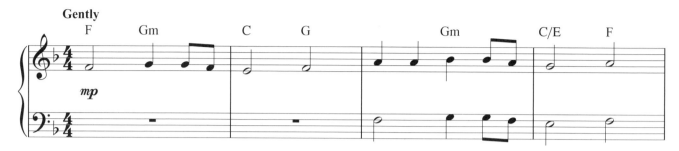

Fa - ther, I a - dore You, Lay my life be - fore You, How I love ___ You.

Je - sus, I a - dore You, Lay my life be -

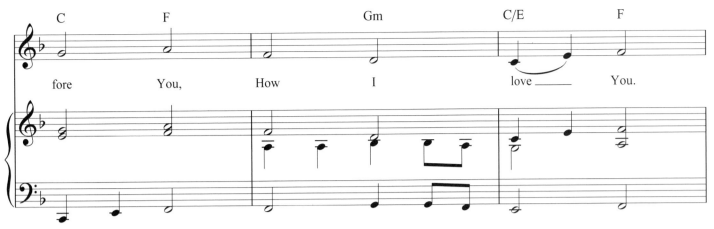

fore You, How I love _____ You.

Spir - it, I a - dore You, Lay my life be -

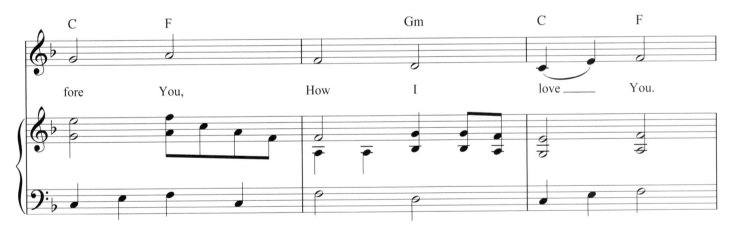

fore You, How I love _____ You.

Here I Am to Worship
(Light of the World)

Words and Music by
Tim Hughes

9

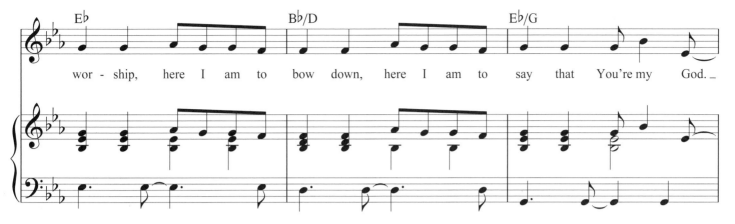

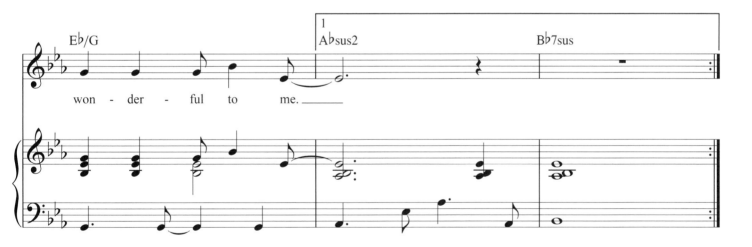

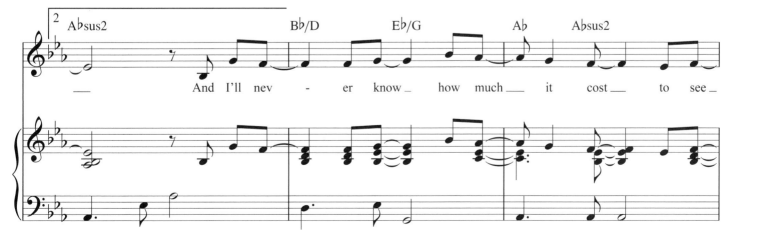

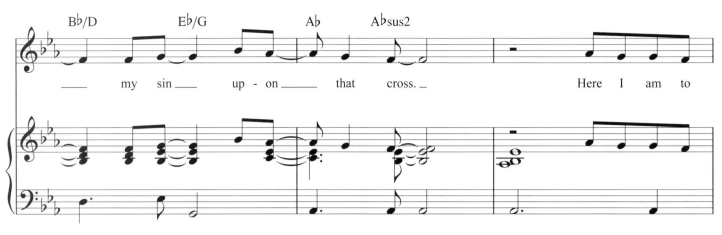

_____ my sin _____ up - on _____ that cross. _____ Here I am to

wor - ship, here I am to bow down, here I am to say that You're my God. _____

_____ You're al - to - geth - er love - ly, al - to - geth - er wor - thy, al - to - geth - er

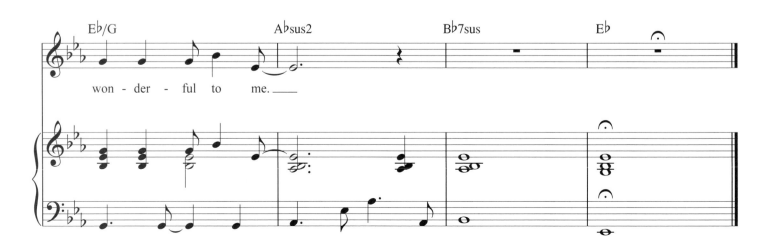

won - der - ful to me. _____

He Is Exalted

Words and Music by
Twila Paris

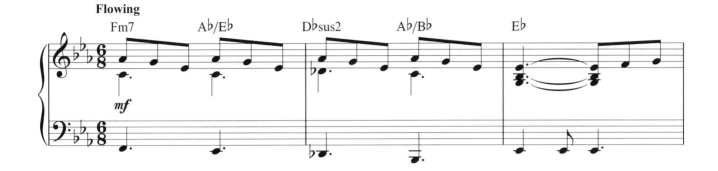

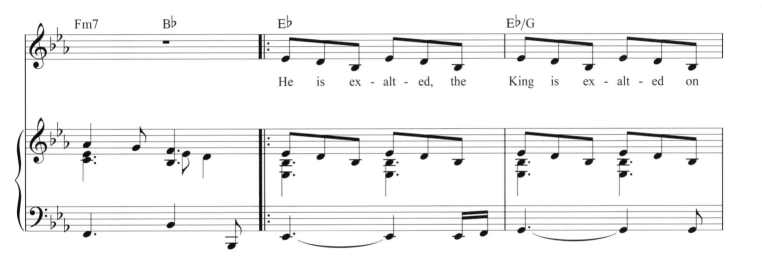

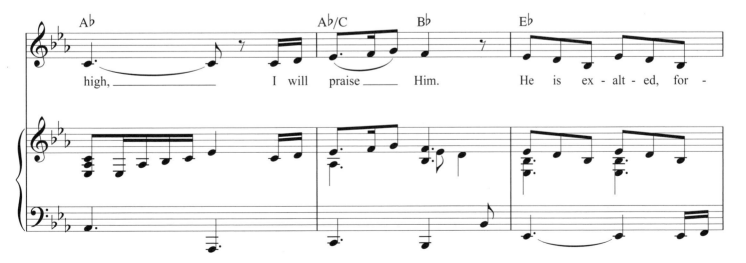

12

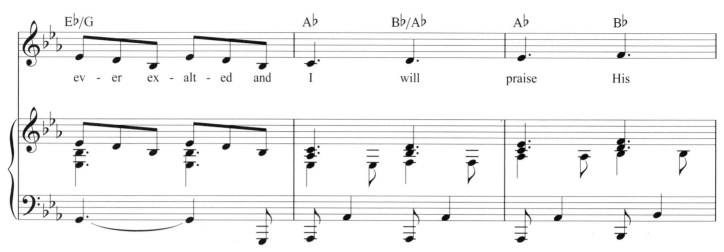

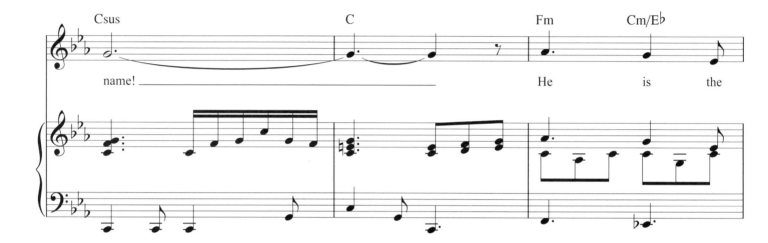

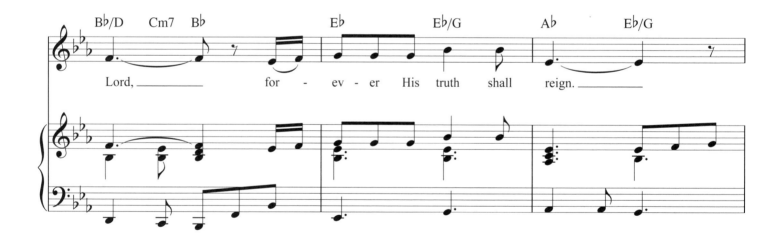

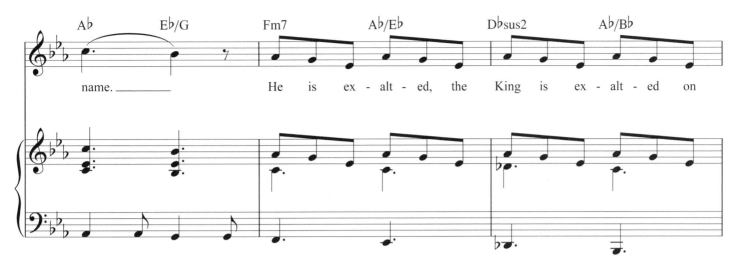

name. _____ He is ex - alt - ed, the King is ex - alt - ed on

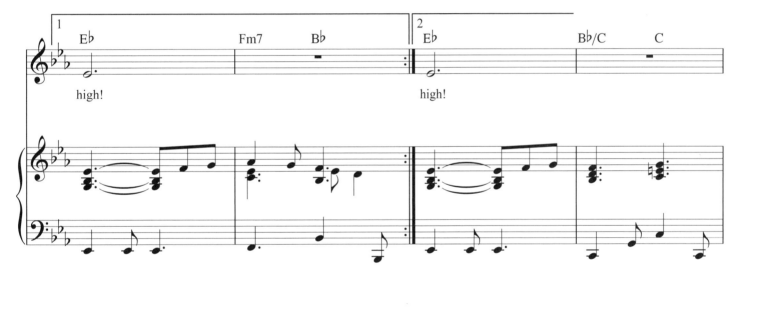

high!   high!

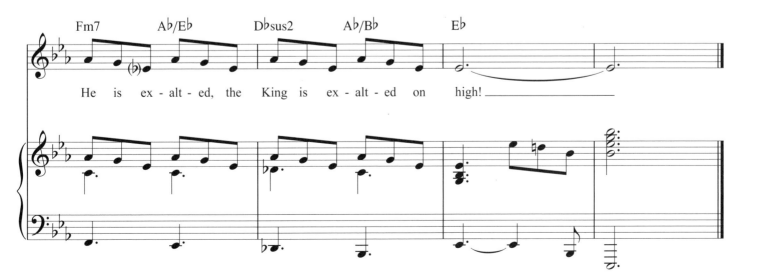

He is ex - alt - ed, the King is ex - alt - ed on high! _____

How Great Is Our God

Words and Music by Chris Tomlin,
Jesse Reeves and Ed Cash

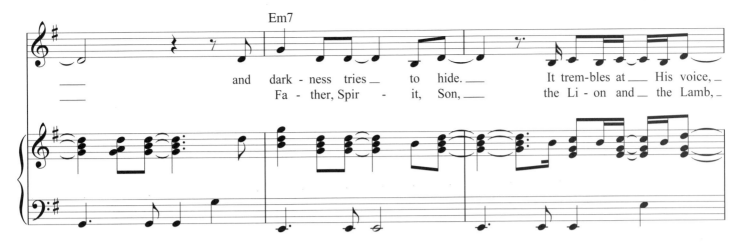

16

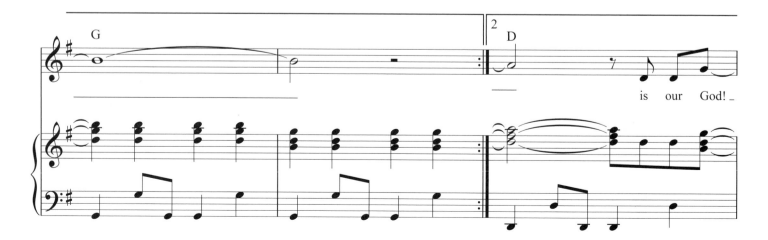

How great _____ is our God!

Sing with me: _____ How great is our God! _

_____ And all _____ will see how great, how great _____ is our God! _

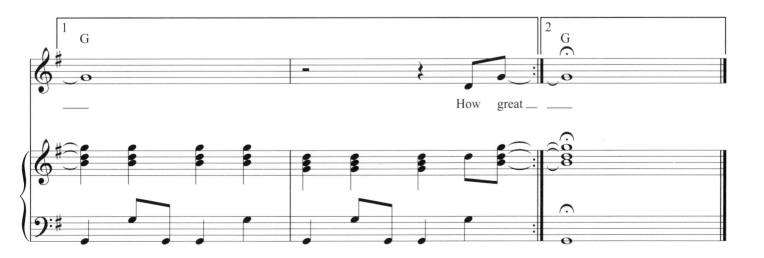

_____ How great _____ _____

Step By Step

Words and Music by
David Strasser "Beaker"

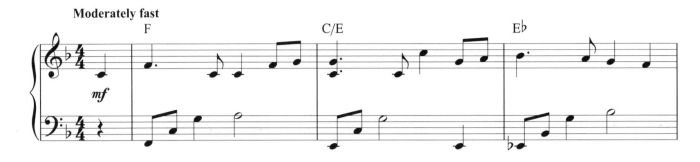

Moderately fast

O God, You are my __ God, and I will ev - er praise __

You. O God, You are my __ God, and I will ev - er praise __

You. I will seek You in the morn - ing, and I will learn to walk in Your __

Gm   B♭/C   F   C/E   C   B♭/D   C

ways. _____ And step by step You'll lead ___ me, and I will fol-low You all of my ___

1 F   B♭/D   C   2 F   Dm

days.   O days. And I will fol-low You all of my ___

Csus   C   B♭   Eb   B♭/C

days,   and I will fol-low You all of my ___ days. _____ And

F/C   C   B♭/D   C   F

step by step You'll lead ___ me, and I will fol-low You all of my ___ days.

rit.

10,000 Reasons
(Bless the Lord)

Words and Music by Jonas Myrin
and Matt Redman

Moderate Ballad

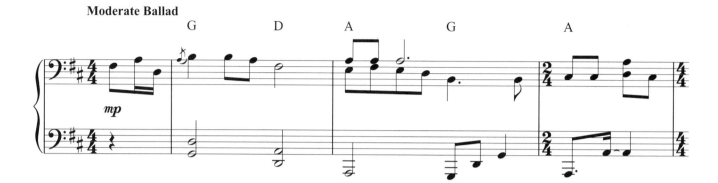

Bless the Lord, O my soul, O_____ my soul.

Wor-ship His ho - ly name.___ Sing like nev - er be - fore,

O my soul. I'll wor-ship Your ho - ly name. ___

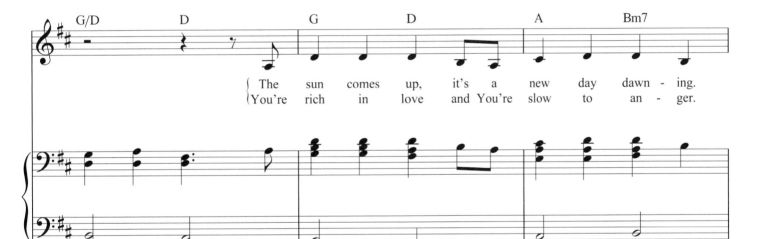

The sun comes up, it's a new day dawn - ing.
You're rich in love and You're slow to an - ger.

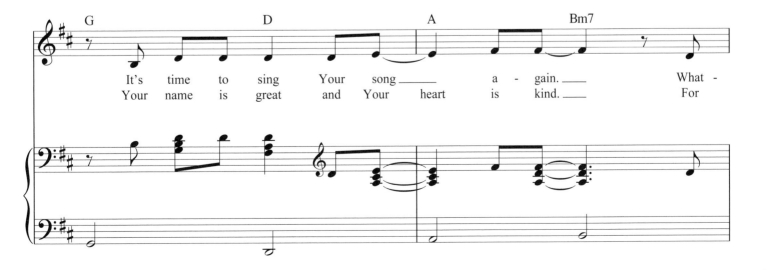

It's time to sing Your song ___ a - gain. ___ What -
Your name is great and Your heart is kind. ___ For

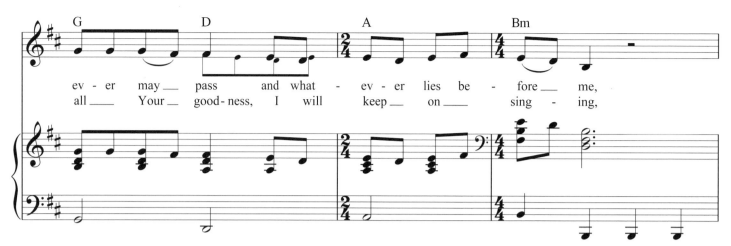

ev - er may __ pass and what - ev - er lies be - fore __ me,
all __ Your __ good - ness, I will keep __ on __ sing - ing,

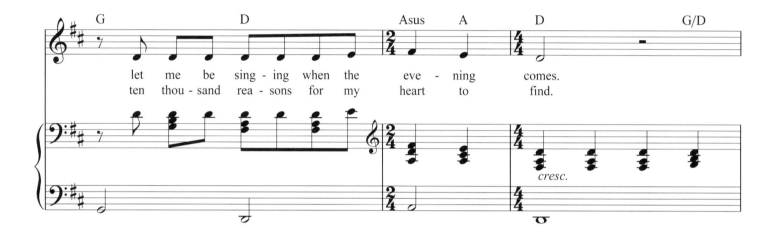

let me be sing - ing when the eve - ning comes.
ten thou - sand rea - sons for my heart to find.

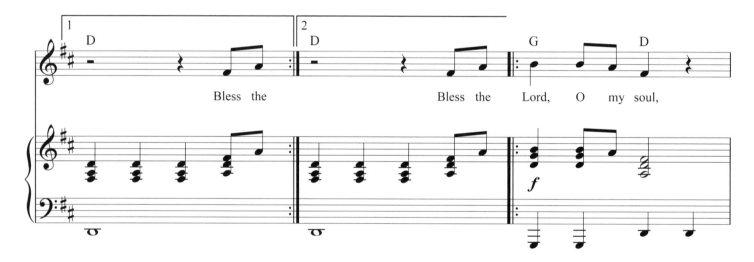

Bless the

Bless the Lord, O my soul,

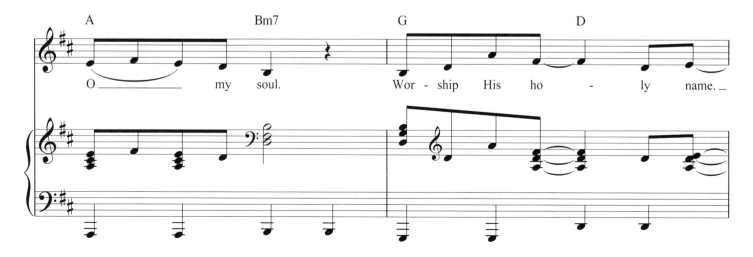

O _____ my soul. Wor - ship His ho - ly name. __

There Is a Redeemer

Words and Music by
Melody Green

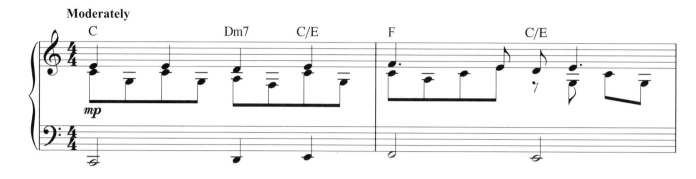

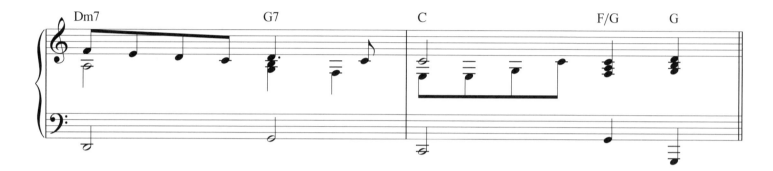

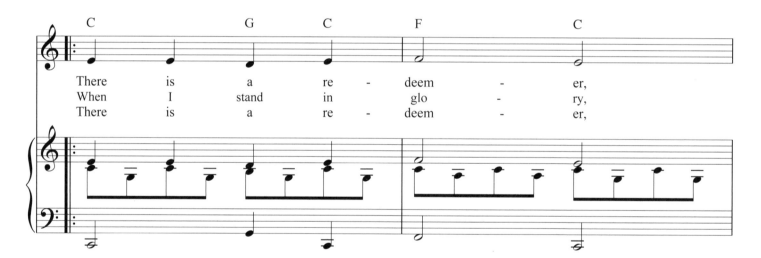

There is a re - deem - er,
When I stand in glo - ry,
There is a re - deem - er,

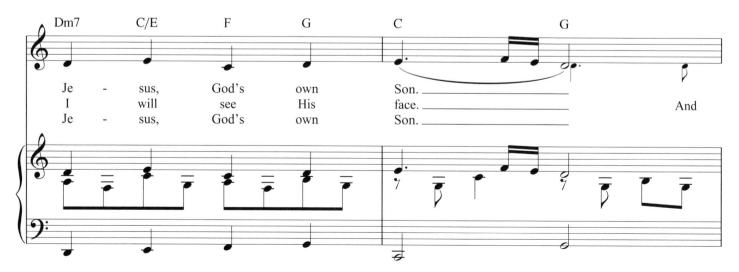

Je - sus, God's own Son.
I will see His face.
Je - sus, God's own Son. And

25

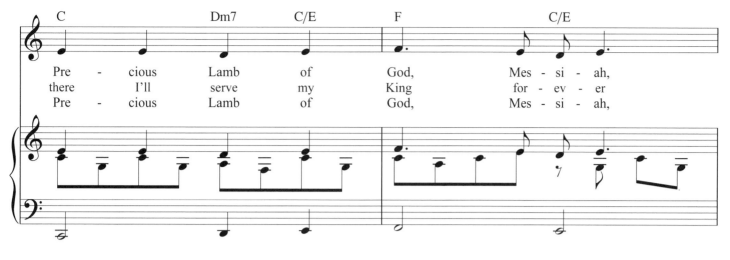

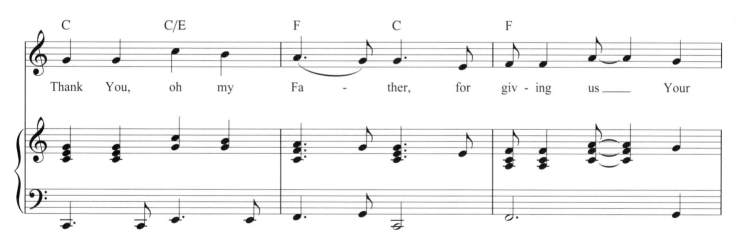

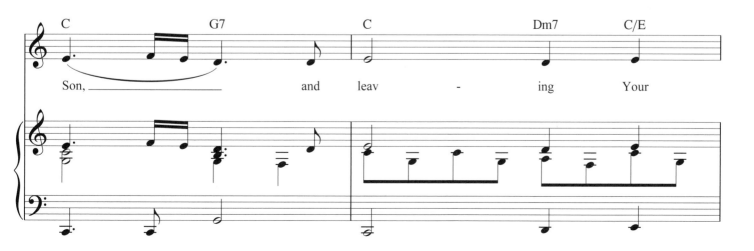

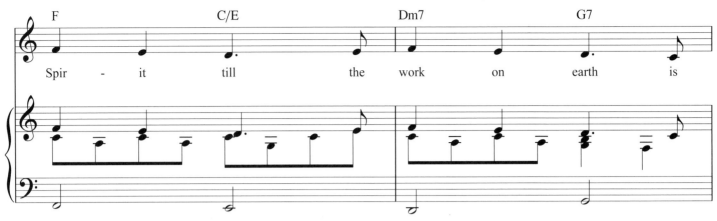

Spir - it till the work on earth is

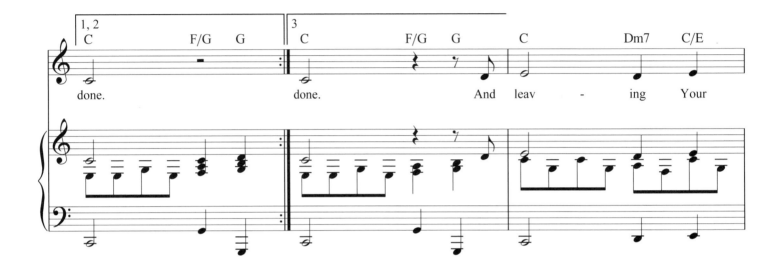

done. done. And leav - ing Your

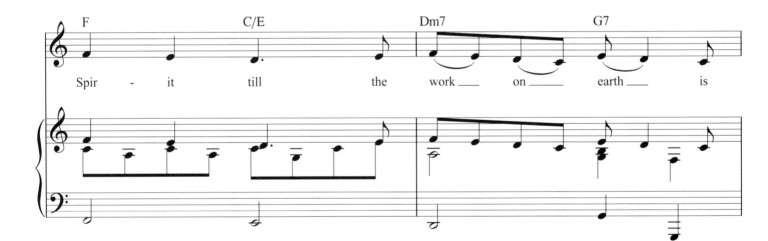

Spir - it till the work on earth is

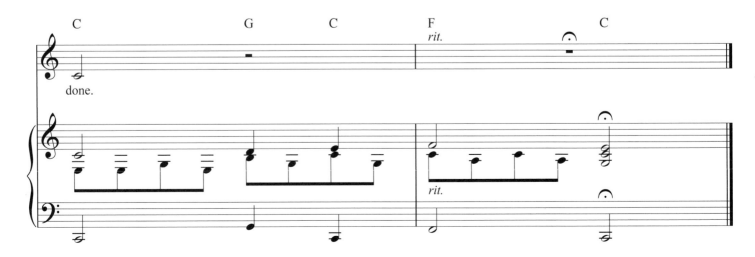

done.

The page has been left blank to facilitate page turns.

We Fall Down

Words and Music by
Chris Tomlin

Worshipfully

We fall down, we lay our crowns at the feet of Je-

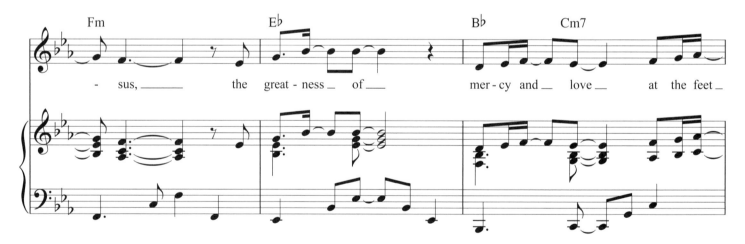

-sus, the great-ness of mer-cy and love at the feet

of Je - sus. And we cry, "Ho - ly, ho - ly, ho-

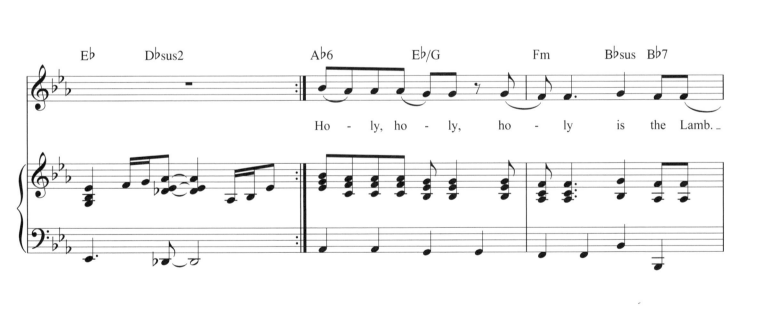

We Will Glorify

Words and Music by
Twila Paris

We will glo-ri-fy the King of kings; we will glo-ri-fy the Lamb. We will glo-ri-fy the Lord of lords, who __ is the great I Am.

Lord Je - ho - va reigns in maj - es - ty, we will bow be - fore His
He is Lord of heav - en, Lord of earth; He is Lord of all who

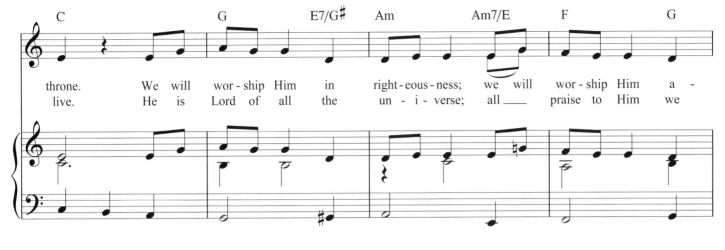

throne. We will wor-ship Him in right-eous-ness; we will wor-ship Him a -
live. He is Lord of all the un - i -verse; all ___ praise to Him we

lone.

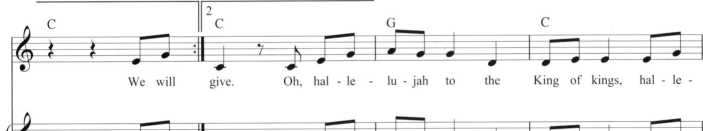

We will give. Oh, hal - le - lu-jah to the King of kings, hal - le -

lu - jah to the Lamb. Hal - le - lu-jah to the Lord of lords, who ___

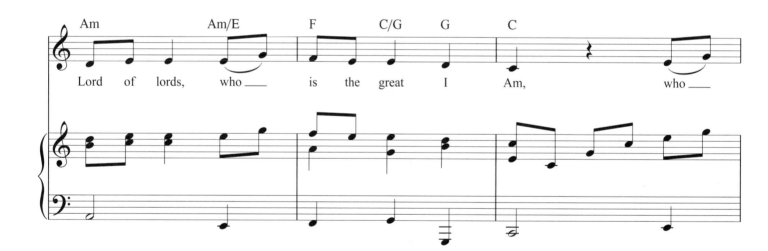